THE WORD DETECTIVE

First published in 1982
Usborne Publishing Ltd
83-85 Saffron Hill
London EC1N 8RT, England

© Usborne Publishing Ltd 1982

Printed in Great Britain

The name of Usborne and the device are trademarks of Usborne Publishing Ltd.

The Word Detectives

A Noun is the name of anything. It can be the name of a thing, like a <u>door</u>, a place like a <u>castle</u> or a person, like a <u>man</u>.

Inspector Noun

A Verb is always busy and tells you about what is happening. <u>Walks</u>, <u>runs</u> and <u>barks</u> are all Verbs.

Sergeant Verb

A Pronoun takes the place of a Noun. <u>He</u> instead of a man, <u>she</u> instead of a girl, <u>it</u> instead of a door. A Pronoun also tells you when a thing belongs to someone, like <u>mine</u>, <u>hers</u> or <u>its</u>.

Detective Pronoun

An Adjective tells you something else about a noun. The words underlined are adjectives: a <u>green</u> door, a <u>tall</u> man, an <u>old</u> castle.

Detective Adjective

An Adverb tells you more about the way something is being done, like walks <u>slowly</u>, runs <u>away</u> or barks <u>loudly</u>.

Detective Adverb

A Preposition goes before a Noun or Pronoun and tells you more about them, such as <u>behind</u> the man, <u>into</u> the castle, or the dog went <u>with</u> him.

Detective Preposition

These are the six Word Detectives. You will find them throughout this book, catching all sorts of thieves, spies and smugglers. When you see one of these Detectives, then the single words on that page will all be Nouns, Adjectives, Verbs, Adverbs, Adjectives, Pronouns or Prepositions.

About this book

This book is both exciting and unusual. In a very entertaining way, it helps children to understand the meaning of nouns, verbs, adverbs, adjectives, prepositions and pronouns. Because these are so cleverly woven into into the stories and so clearly illustrated, children will soon learn about their place and function in the English language.

Those children who are not old enough to appreciate this aspect of The Word Detective Book will, nevertheless, enjoy every page, for each one is packed with pictures and words, people to find and paths to follow. It is a book for all the family to enjoy.

Betty Root
Centre for the Teaching of Reading
University of Reading, England

Spot the mouse
On every picture across two pages there is a mouse. Can you find it?

THE WORD DETECTIVE

WORDS AND SENTENCES FOR BEGINNERS

Heather Amery
Illustrated by Colin King

Consultant: Betty Root

Inspector Noun and the market mystery

market

vegetables   fruit

Noun goes to market to find a thief.

cherries

"Who is eating the cherries

strawberries

and the strawberries

raspberries

and the raspberries?"

pineapple

He looks at a pineapple,

melon

drops a melon

apple

and eats an apple.

oranges

He walks past the oranges

lemons

and the lemons

apricots

and the apricots.

pears

He looks at the pears,

grapes

at the grapes

bananas

and the bananas.

peach

He stops to squeeze a peach,

grapefruit

buy a grapefruit

plums

and some plums.

peas

"Who has been eating the peas

beans

and the beans

lettuce

and the lettuce?"

potatoes

Noun looks at the potatoes

carrots

and the carrots

cabbages

and the cabbages.

tomato

He steps on a tomato,

mushrooms

knocks down some mushrooms

watercress

and kicks over the watercress.

turnips

He peers round the turnips

sprouts

and the sprouts

beetroot

and crawls past the beetroot.

celery

He walks past the celery,

radishes

looks at the radishes

onions

and the onions.

leek

He slips on a leek,

cauliflower

trips over a cauliflower

thieves

and finds the thieves.

5

Inspector Noun and the missing diamonds

ship

Noun drives to the ship.

gang plank

He walks up the gang plank

captain

and talks to the captain.

diamonds

thief

woman

The captain says some diamonds have been stolen by a thief.   But a woman saw him.

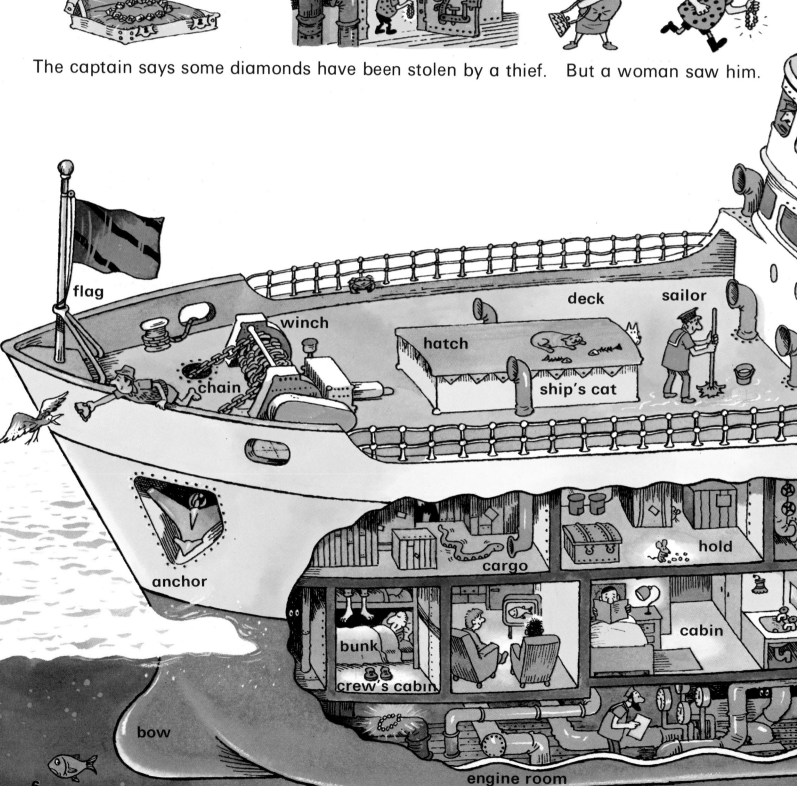

flag

winch

deck

sailor

hatch

ship's cat

chain

anchor

cargo

hold

bunk

cabin

crew's cabin

bow

engine room

6

deck

Noun creeps along the deck

man

and catches the man.

pockets

But his pockets are empty.

The thief has hidden the diamonds in the ship.
Can you find them?

mast

funnel

gull

bridge

saloon

lifeboats

deckchair

railings

chef

kitchen

dining room

waiter

stern

bathroom

shower

stairs

port holes

rudder

propellor

engineer

ladder

Sergeant Verb has a busy day

sleep

Verb sleeps in bed.

wake up

He wakes up

climb

and climbs out of bed.

turn

He turns on the taps,

wash

washes his hands

rub

and rubs his face.

clean

He cleans his teeth,

take

takes off his pajamas

put

and puts on his clothes.

brush

He brushes his hair.

slide

He slides down the banister

eat

and then eats his breakfast.

drink

He drinks his coffee,

read

reads a newspaper

drop

and drops a plate.

feed

He feeds the canary,

close

closes the window

open

and opens the door.

drive

Verb drives his car,

walk

walks into his office

write

and writes a letter.

talk

He talks on the telephone,

tell

tells Noun about a robbery

run

and runs out to his car.

look

He looks at a window,

see

sees a footprint

search

and searches for Bodger, the burglar.

chase

Verb chases Bodger,

catch

catches him

fight

and they fight.

kick

Bodger kicks Verb,

hit

Verb hits Bodger

fall

and he falls down.

pick

Verb picks him up,

take

takes him to the police station

lock

and locks him in.

Inspector Noun and the prize bull

Three silly robbers try to steal a prize bull.
Which gates does Inspector Noun go through to catch them?

farmhouse

barn

scarecrow

hay

garden

logs

cart

farmer

Inspector Noun

farmer's wife

pigs

pigsty

cock

turkeys

piglets

hen house

hens

goslings

chicks

geese

farm worker

ducks

pond

ducklings

straw

stable

sheep

lambs

goat

orchard

fox

shed

silo

tractor

trailer

plough

elevator

rabbits

water trough

yard

cows

shepherd

cowshed

sheepdog

calves

donkey

bull

horses

landrover

foal

Inspector Noun and the factory spies

factory

Noun is on watch outside a factory. He sees two spies run out.

street

He follows them down the street,

gates

through the gates

park

and into the park.

lake

He walks past the lake

swings

and the swings

band

and the band.

school

The spies are near a school.

railings

Noun looks through some railings and sees them in the playground.

playground

church

He chases them past the church,

cinema

round the cinema

hotel

and into a hotel.

café

traffic lights

crossing

He finds the spies at a café. Off they go to the traffic lights and walk across the crossing.

bus stop

They wait at a bus stop.

lamp post

Noun runs round a street lamp

statue

and hides behind a statue.

bus

The spies miss the bus

hospital

and walk on past the hospital

hole

and a hole in the road.

drill

They watch the man with a drill,

digger

look at a digger

roller

and a roller.

pipes

They jump over some pipes

bricks

and some bricks.

policeman

Then they see Noun with a policeman.

office

They hurry into an office,

stairs

up the stairs

fire escape

and on to the fire escape.

roof

flag pole

chimney

Noun chases them on to the roof, round a flag pole and at last traps them by a chimney.

Inspector Noun goes flying

Inspector Noun drives to the airport. He is looking for a smuggler.

ticket

His ticket is checked.

customs

He goes through the customs

passport

and has his passport stamped.

lounge

He waits in the lounge.

pass

He is given his boarding pass.

passengers

He looks at the other passengers.

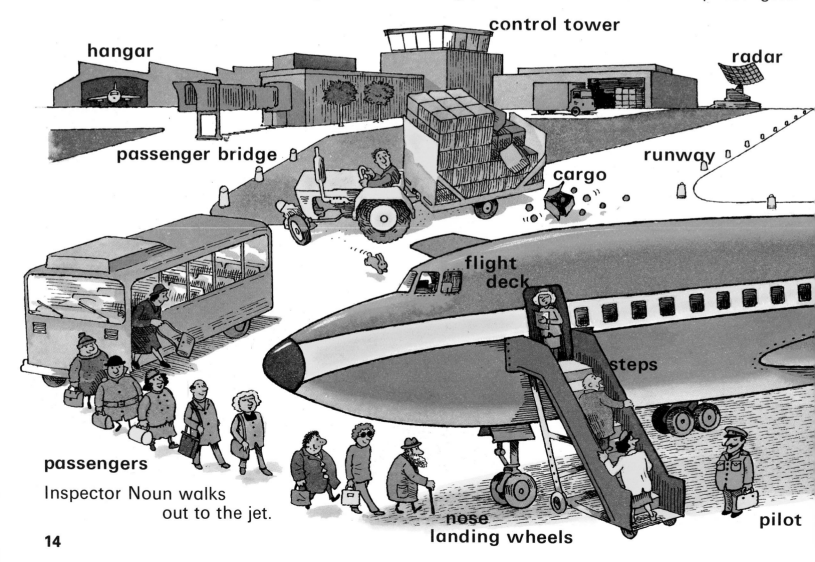

control tower

hangar

radar

passenger bridge

runway

cargo

flight deck

steps

passengers

Inspector Noun walks out to the jet.

nose
landing wheels

pilot

cabin

He walks down the cabin

seat

and finds his seat.

safety belt

He fastens his safety belt.

runway

The jet speeds down the runway

air

and takes off into the air.

flight deck

Noun goes to the flight deck.

pilot

He talks to the pilot,

controls

looks at the controls

gangway

and walks down the gangway.

gold bars

He sees the gold bars,

stewardess

so he whispers to the stewardess

smuggler

and arrests the smuggler.

tail

fuel tanker

wing

engine

baggage train

main landing wheels

stewardess

suitcase

Inspector Noun in the disguise shop

Noun and his assistant go to a shop to choose disguises for a special mission.
How many disguises do they try on?

boots

shoes

slippers

hats

caps

socks

ties

trousers

kilts

shirts

jeans

gloves

coats

jerseys

anoraks

dungarees

suits

raincoats

wigs

false noses

pajamas

uniforms

beards

moustaches

dressing gowns

shorts

tee-shirts

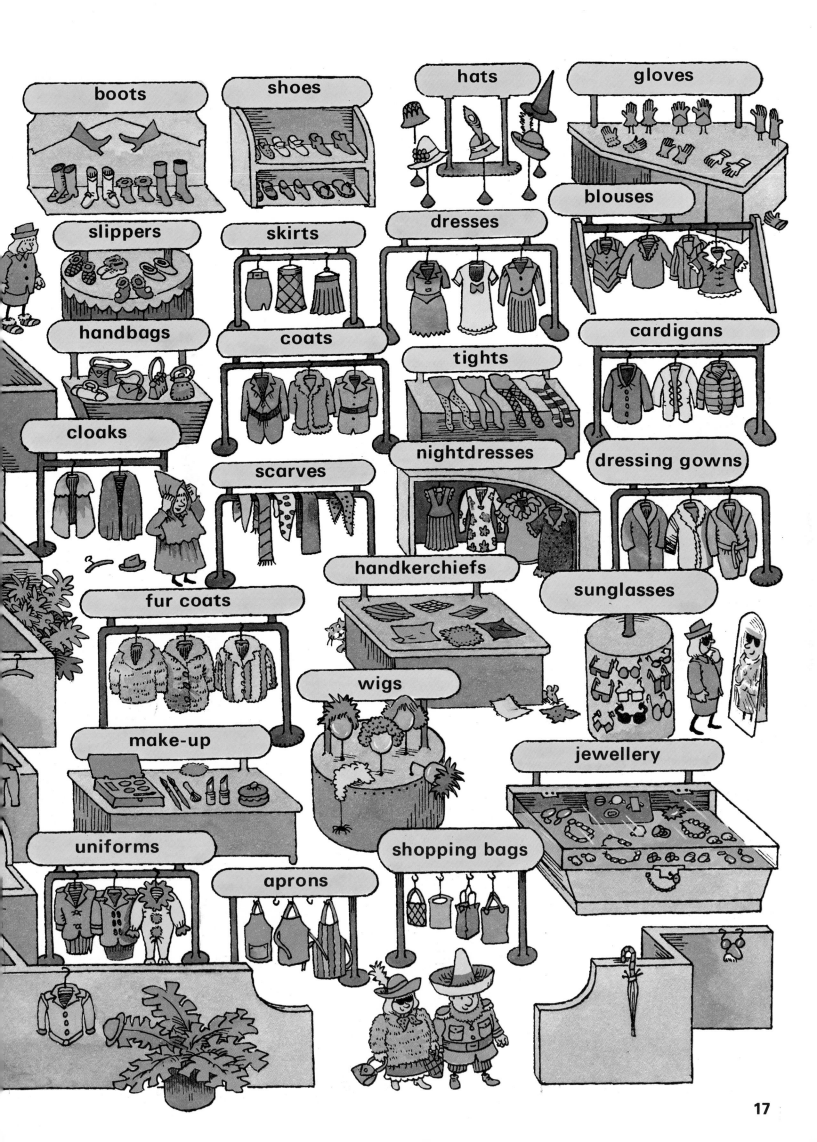

boots
shoes
hats
gloves
blouses
slippers
skirts
dresses
handbags
coats
tights
cardigans
cloaks
nightdresses
dressing gowns
scarves
handkerchiefs
sunglasses
fur coats
wigs
make-up
jewellery
uniforms
shopping bags
aprons

Inspector Noun and the supermarket gang

Noun goes to the supermarket. He is looking for some food robbers.

bread

He walks past the bread

butter

and the butter

cheese

and looks at the cheese.

milk

He goes past the milk

yogurt

and the yogurt

eggs

and drops some eggs.

ham

Noun looks at the ham

bacon

and the bacon

fish

and crawls past the fish.

flour

He peers round the flour

sugar

and the sugar

chocolate

and the chocolate.

honey

He stands by the honey,

jam

looks at the jam

sweets

and chooses some sweets.

cakes

He runs past the cakes

cookies

and the cookies

bread rolls

and steps over the bread rolls.

cans

He knocks over cans

bottles

and bottles

jars

and jars.

freezer

He rests by the freezer,

basket

kicks over a basket

boxes

and some boxes.

meat

Noun finds some meat,

chicken

a chicken

sausages

and some sausages.

cash desk

He runs past the cash desk,

bags

jumps over some bags

sacks

and some sacks.

robbers

Then he catches the robbers.

cart

He puts them in a cart

dog pound

and takes them to the dog pound.

Detective Preposition and the haunted castle

Detective Preposition goes to the castle. Crooks have hidden some treasure there.

at

He looks at the moat,

over

walks over the drawbridge

under

and under the gatehouse.

for

He is searching for the treasure.

on

He switches on his flashlight

between

and shines it between two cannons.

by

As he stops by a pillar,

of

he hears the sound of footsteps

into

and looks into a room.

behind

A ghost appears behind him.

with

He shakes with fright

from

and runs away from the ghost.

down

He jumps down the stairs,

through

falls through the floor

up

and tries to climb up the wall.

Detective Pronoun to the rescue

When Preposition does not come back, Detective Pronoun goes to the haunted castle.

she

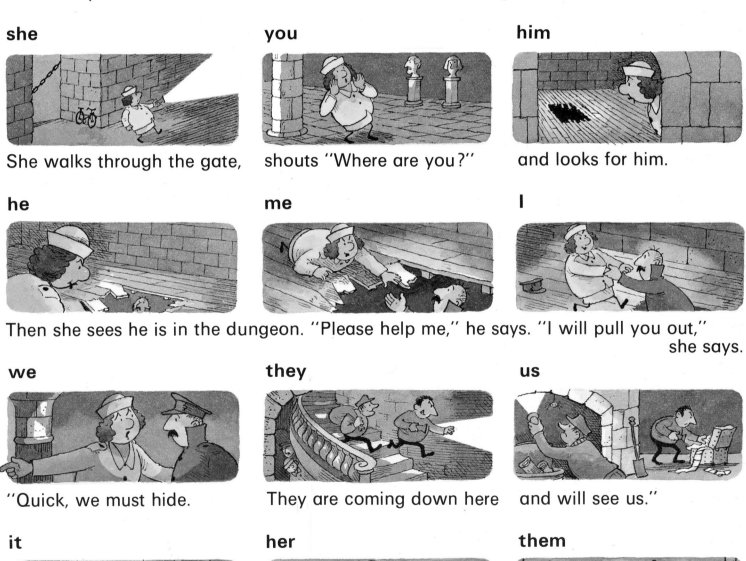

She walks through the gate,

you

shouts "Where are you?"

him

and looks for him.

he

me

I

Then she sees he is in the dungeon. "Please help me," he says. "I will pull you out," she says.

we

"Quick, we must hide.

they

They are coming down here

us

and will see us."

it

"We have found it," says a crook.

her

Suddenly they see her

them

but Pronoun arrests them.

Inspector Noun and the kidnappers

One night ten spies creep into a hotel to kidnap a famous scientist.

When they hear Inspector Noun coming, they hide. Can you find them all?

girls

boys

scientist

bedroom

shower

bedroom

toilet

clock

lamp

mirror

television

reception

coal

fireplace

books

bookcase

cushion

armchair

shelves

cupboard

wine

store room

beer

boiler

Inspector Noun chases the crooks

prison

Two crooks escape from prison. Noun runs after them.

tandem

They ride away on a tandem.

bicycle

Noun chases them on a bicycle.

scooter

They jump on a scooter.

roller skates

Noun follows them on roller skates.

car

The crooks steal a car.

taxi

Noun hires a taxi.

truck

They drive off in a truck.

van

Noun follows them in a van.

plane

The crooks fly off in a plane.

helicopter

Noun chases them in a helicopter.

parachute

They come down by parachute.

balloon

Noun lands in a balloon.

train

They catch a train.

racing car

Noun drives after them in a racing car.

motor boat

They steal a motor boat.

sailing boat

Noun follows in a sailing boat.

rowing boat

They jump into a rowing boat.

kayak

Noun paddles after them in a kayak.

horse trailer

They steal a horse trailer.

fire engine

Noun has a ride on a fire engine.

motor bike

They crash a motorbike.

ambulance

Noun catches them and takes them away in an ambulance.

Verb School

Good detectives have to be able to do all sorts of things.
Here are lots of Verbs at a secret training school.
But there are six crooks watching them.
Can you find them?

row

fly

skate

build

cut

blow

fall

stand

race

sing

play

conduct

paint

WAIT

wait

swing

dance

think

hop

cook

knit

make

sew

stop

STOP

27

Detective Adverb and the meat thief

One day Detective Adverb saw a man stealing some meat. This is what he saw.

slowly

loudly

sadly

A dog was walking slowly along, sniffing loudly for food.   Then he sat down sadly.

suddenly

soon

happily

A man suddenly grabbed some meat and the dog soon ate it. He wagged his tail happily.

gently

angrily

quickly

The man gently patted the dog. The butcher shouted angrily and the man ran quickly away.

fiercely

almost

away

The dog barked fiercely.   The butcher almost caught it   but it ran away.

28

Detective Adjective's Report

Detective Adjective saw the dog and the man. This is her description of them.

thin

The dog had a thin head,

pointed

pointed ears

brown

and brown eyes.

black

It had a black coat,

long

a long tail

red

and wore a red collar.

round

The man had a round face,

curly

curly hair

grey

and a grey beard.

green

He wore a green hat,

old

an old coat

white

and a white shirt.

blue

He had blue trousers,

yellow

yellow socks

big

and big shoes.

Inspector Noun and the smugglers

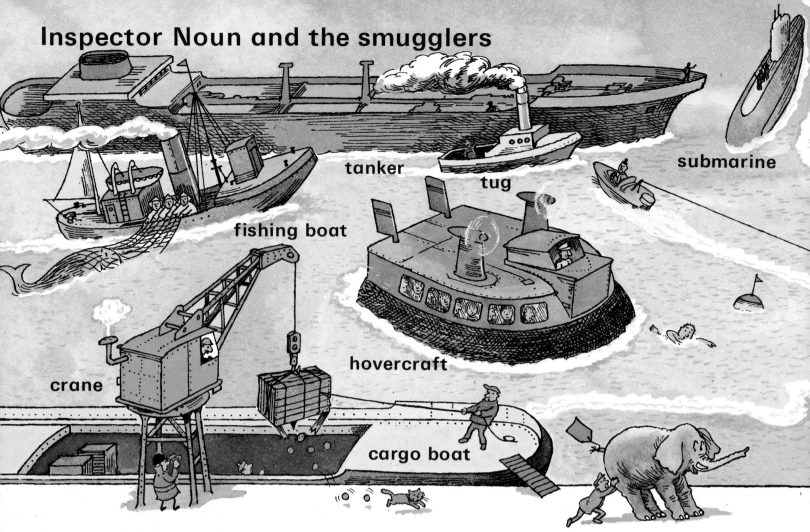

fishing boat

tanker

tug

submarine

crane

hovercraft

cargo boat

Inspector Noun is waiting for some smugglers.   He wants to find their hide-out.

motor boat

smugglers

beach

He sees a motor boat   and watches the smugglers.   He follows them along the beach.

sand castle

bucket

umbrella

They walk past a sandcastle,   kick over a bucket   and knock down an umbrella.

spade

ball

picnic

One steps on a spade,   another kicks a ball.   The smugglers stop for a picnic.

wreck

harbour wall

hydrofoil

water skier

car ferry

buoy

crates

warehouse

pebbles

Noun sits on the pebbles.

crab

He picks up a crab

rock pool

and puts it into a rock pool.

rocks

He follows the men to the rocks,

sea weed

slips on some seaweed

lighthouse

and reaches the lighthouse.

cliff

He climbs up the cliff,

tunnel

crawls into a tunnel,

cave

and finds the smugglers' cave.

Inspector Noun in danger

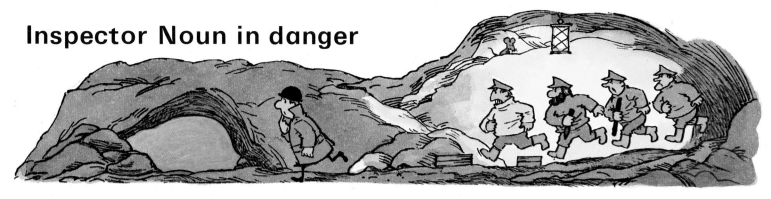

Noun finds the smugglers in their cave. But they see he is alone and start to chase him.

road

He runs away along a road,

bridge

crosses over a bridge

cross roads

and reaches a crossroads.

sign post

Noun stops to read a sign post,

path

runs on down a path

hedge

and crawls through a hedge.

trees

He runs towards some trees.

river

Then he comes to a river

raft

and paddles across on a raft.

waterfall

He just misses a waterfall,

hill

hurries up a hill

fence

and jumps over a fence.

canal

Noun stops by a canal,

barge

leaps on to a barge

lock

and jumps off again at a lock.

gate

Noun climbs over a gate,

tents

hurries past some tents

rope

and trips over a rope.

motorhome

He runs past a motorhome,

stream

reaches a stream and crosses

stepping stones

over by the stepping stones.

dam

He dashes across a dam,

windmill

past a windmill

forest

and into a forest.

mountain

He starts to climb a mountain,

cable car

then rides in a cable car

snow

and steps out into the snow.

skis

He tries on some skis,

toboggan

slides down on a toboggan

wall

and then climbs over a wall.

room

Noun runs into a dark room

light

and switches on the light.

police station

The smugglers are caught
in a police station.

Inspector Noun goes to the zoo

At the zoo the lion has escaped from its cage. Which path does Noun go along to find it?

cage

keeper

Inspector Noun

polar bear

snakes

elephant

camel

seals

kangaroo

tiger

giraffe

penguins

owl

ostriches

flamingos

crocodiles

hippopotamus

rhinoceros

lion

zebra

buffalo

reindeer

panda

goats

bears

porcupine

pelican

beaver

monkeys

parrot   toucan

wolf

tortoise

eagle

Inspector Noun looks for clues

Noun opens the door of his office. "Someone has been in here," he thinks, and looks for clues.

floor

He looks at the floor,

drawer

finds an open drawer

watch

and picks up a watch.

key

He finds a key

handkerchief

and a handkerchief

flashlight

and a flashlight.

pen

Someone has used his pen,

stamp

stolen a stamp

envelope

and opened an envelope.

notebook

computer

calculator

Someone has read his notebook, played with his computer and dropped his calculator.

pencil

drink

sandwich

Someone has broken his pencil, finished his drink and eaten his sandwich.

Then he looks in his cupboard and finds the burglar.

Inspector Noun, the space spy-catcher

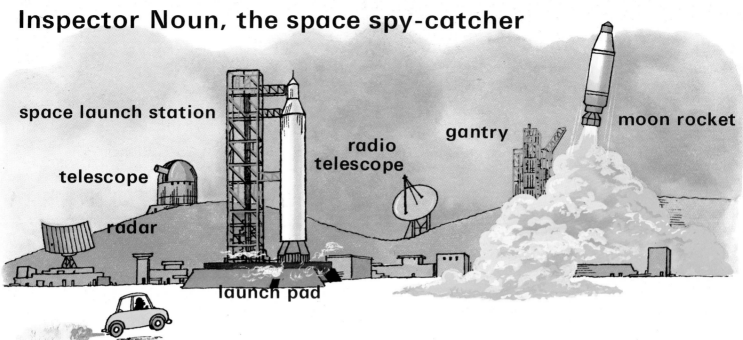

Noun reaches the space launch station just as a rocket blasts off. He knows there is a spy on board.

space suit

He puts on a space suit,

astronauts

meets two astronauts

launch pad

and is taken to the launch pad.

space craft

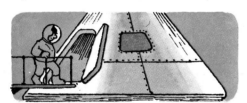

He goes into the space craft,

couch

lies on a couch

rocket

and the rocket takes off.

earth

He sees the earth below

sun

and looks at the sun

stars

and the stars.

space shuttle

He whizzes past a space shuttle,

satellite

a satellite

space station

and a space station.

lunar module

moon buggy

Noun lands on the moon. The other rocket is there.

moon buggy

He rides on a moon buggy,

moon dust

sees footprints in the moon dust

moon rock

and catches the spy by a moon rock.

space

He takes off into space again.

meteor

The module is hit by a meteor.

space walk

Noun goes for a space walk.

antenna

He mends an antenna.

orbit

sea

The module goes into orbit and they splash down in the sea.

nose cone

They climb out of the nose cone.

frogmen

Frogmen are there to help them.

mission

The mission is safely over.

More Detective Work

Here are some detectives at work. How many Nouns and Verbs can you find?

garage

tree

ices

steal

car

window

van

apartments

climb

push

butcher

bank

dog

shop

sausages

run

robber

bicycle

play

apple

policeman

fountain

elephant

pull

Words in order

This is a list of all the single words in the pictures. They are in the same order as the alphabet. After each word is number. This is the page number. On that page you will find the word and a picture.

a

airport, 14
alarm clock, 37
almost, 28
ambulance, 25
anchor, 6
angrily, 28
anoraks, 16
antenna, 39
apple, 4
apricots, 7
aprons, 17, 22
armchair, 23
astronauts, 38
at, 20
away, 28
axe, 37

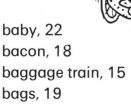

b

baby, 22
bacon, 18
baggage train, 15
bags, 19
bags, shopping, 17

baker, 13
balcony, 22
ball, 30
balloon, 25
bananas, 4
band, 12
bandages, 37
barge, 32
barn, 10
basket, 19
bathroom, 7, 22
beach, 30
beans, 5
beard s, 16
bears, 35
beaver, 35
bed, 22
bedroom, 22, 23
beer, 23
beetroot, 5
behind, 20
belt, safety, 15
between, 20
bicycle, 24
big, 29
bike, motor, 25
binoculars, 37
black, 29
blanket, 22
blouses, 17
blow, 27
blue, 29
boat, cargo, 30
boat, fishing, 30
boat, motor, 25, 30
boat, rowing, 25
boat, sailing, 25
boat, tug, 30
boiler, 23
bookcase, 23, 36
books, 23, 37
boots, 16, 17
bottles, 19
bow (of ship), 7
boxes, 19
boys, 23
bread, 18
bricks, 13

bridge, 7, 32
bridge, passenger, 14
brown, 29
to brush, 8
a brush, 37
brussel sprouts, 5
bucket, 30
buffalo, 35
buggy, 22
buggy, moon, 39
build, 27
bull, 11
bunk, 6
buoy, 31
bus, 13
bus stop, 13
butcher, 13
butter, 18
by, 20

c

cabbages, 5
cabin, 6, 15
cable car, 33
café, 12
cage, 34
cakes, 19
calculator, 37
calendar, 36
calf, 11
calves, 11
camel, 34
camera, 37
canal, 32
cans, 19
caps, 16
captain, 6
car, 24
car ferry, 31
cardigans, 17
cargo, 6, 14
cargo boat, 30

carpet, 23, 36
carrots, 5
carry, 26
cart, 11, 19
cash desk, 19
castle, 20
cat, 6
catch, 9
cauliflower, 5
cave, 31
celery, 5
chain, 6
chair, 22
chase, 9
cheese, 18
chef, 7
cherries, 4
cherry, 4
chicken, 19
chicks, 10
chimney, 13
chocolate, 18
church, 12
cinema, 12
clean, 8
cliff, 31
climb, 8
cloaks, 17
clock, 23
close, 8
coal, 23
coats, 16, 17
cockerel, 10
command module, 39
computer, 36, 37
conduct, 27
control tower, 14
controls, 15
cook, 27
cooker, 22
cookies, 19
corridor, 22
cot, 22
couch, 38
cows, 11
cowshed, 11
crab, 31
craft, space, 38
crane, 30

crates, 31
crawl, 26
crew's cabin, 6
crocodiles, 34
cross road, 32
crossing, 12
cupboard, 23, 36
cups, 37
curly, 29
curtains, 22
cushion, 23
customs, 14
cut, 27

d

dam, 33
dance, 27
deck, 6, 7
deckchair, 7
desk, 36
desk, cash, 19
diamonds, 6
dig, 26
digger, 13
dining room, 7, 22
dishwasher, 22
dive, 26
dog pound, 19
dog, sheep, 11
donkey, 11
door handle, 36
down, 20
drawer, 36
dress, 14
dresses, 14
dressing gowns, 16, 17
dressing table, 22
drill, 13
to drink, 8
a drink, 37
drive, 9
drop, 8
ducklings, 10

ducks, 10
dungarees, 16
dust, moon, 39

e

eagle, 35
earth, 38, 39
eat, 8
eggs, 18
elephant, 34
elevator, 11, 22
engine, 15
engine room, 6
engineer, 7
envelope, 36

f

factory, 12
fall, 9, 27
false noses, 16
farm worker, 10
farmer, 10
farmer's wife, 10
farmhouse, 10
feed, 8
fence, 32
ferry, car, 31
fiercely, 28
fight, 9
find, 26
fire engine, 25
fire escape, 13
fireplace, 23
first-aid kit, 37
fish, 18
fishing boat, 30

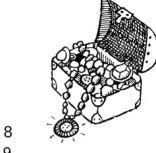

r

rabbits, 11
race, 27
racing car, 25
radar, 14, 38
radiator, 22
radio telescope, 38
radishes, 5
raft, 32
railings, 7, 12
raincoats, 16
raspberries, 4
raspberry, 4
read, 8
reception, 23
record player, 37
records, 37
red, 29
refrigerator, 22
reindeer, 35
rhinoceros, 35
ride, 26
river, 32
road, 32
robbers, 19
rock, moon, 39
rock pool, 31
rocket, 38
rocks, 31
roller, 13
roller skates, 24
roof, 13
room, 33
rope, 33
round, 29
row, 27
rowing boat, 25
rub, 8
rudder, 7
run, 9
runway, 14, 15

s

sacks, 19
sadly, 28

safety belt, 15
safety pins, 37
sailing boat, 25
sailor, 6
saloon, 7
sand castle, 30
sandwich, 37
satellite, 38
saucepans, 22
saucers, 37
sausages, 19
saw, 37
scarecrow, 10
scarves, 17
scissors, 37
school, 12
scientist, 23
scooter, 24
screwdriver, 37
sea, 39
seaweed, 31
seals, 34
search, 9
seat, 15
see, 9
sew, 27
shade, 36
she, 21
shed, 11
sheep, 10
sheep dog, 11
shelf, 23
shelves, 23
shepherd, 11
ship, 6
shirts, 16
shoes, 16, 17
shoot, 26
shopping bags, 17
shorts, 16
shower, 7, 23
shuttle, space, 38
sign post, 32
silo, 11
sing, 27
sink, 22
sit, 26
skate, 26
skates, roller, 24

skier, water, 31
skip, 26
skirts, 17
skis, 33
sleep, 8
slide, 8
slippers, 16, 17
slowly, 28
smile, 26
smugglers, 15, 30
snakes, 34
snow, 33
soap, 22
socks, 16
soon, 28
space, 39
space craft, 38
space launch station, 38
space shuttle, 38
space station, 38
space suit, 38
space walk, 39
spade, 30
spoons, 37
sprouts, 5
stable, 10
stairs, 7, 13, 22
stamps, 36
stand, 27
stars, 38
station, space, 38
station, police, 33
statue, 13
stepping stones, 33
steps, 14
stern (of ship), 7
stewardess, 15
stop, 27
straw, 10
strawberries, 4
strawberry, 4
store room, 23
stream, 33
street, 12
string, 17
submarine, 31
suddenly, 28
sugar, 18
suit, space, 38

t

u

v

w

y

z